Copyright 2015 by Jane Burn.

All rights reserved. No part of this publication may
be reproduced, distributed or transmitted in any form,
or by any means, including photocopying, recording or other
electronic or mechanical methods without the prior written
permission of the author/publisher except in the case of
quotations embodied in reviews and certain
other non-commercial uses permitted by copyright law.

ISBN-13:
978-1519675149

ISBN-10:
1519675143

For Dominic and James

Any similarity to anybody I know, or have known is purely coincidental.

The Pig in The Wig

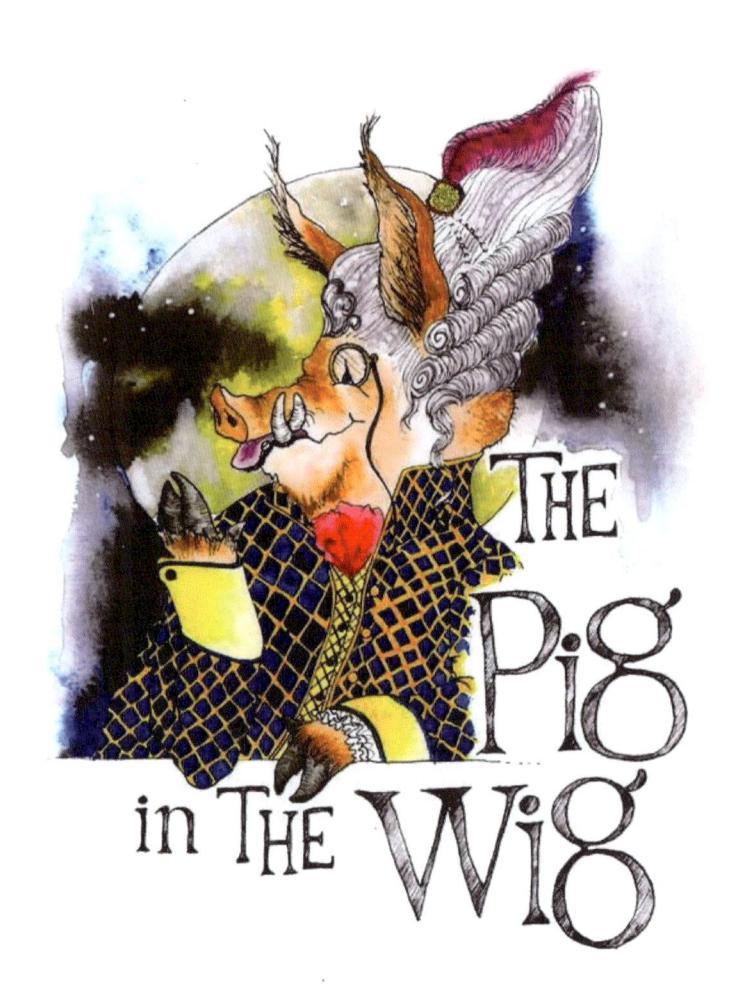

The snuffling pig wears a fluffy white wig.

A fluffy white wig
for a snuffling pig.

The snuffling pig
in the white fluffy
wig has a bed that
is small and some
shoes that are big.

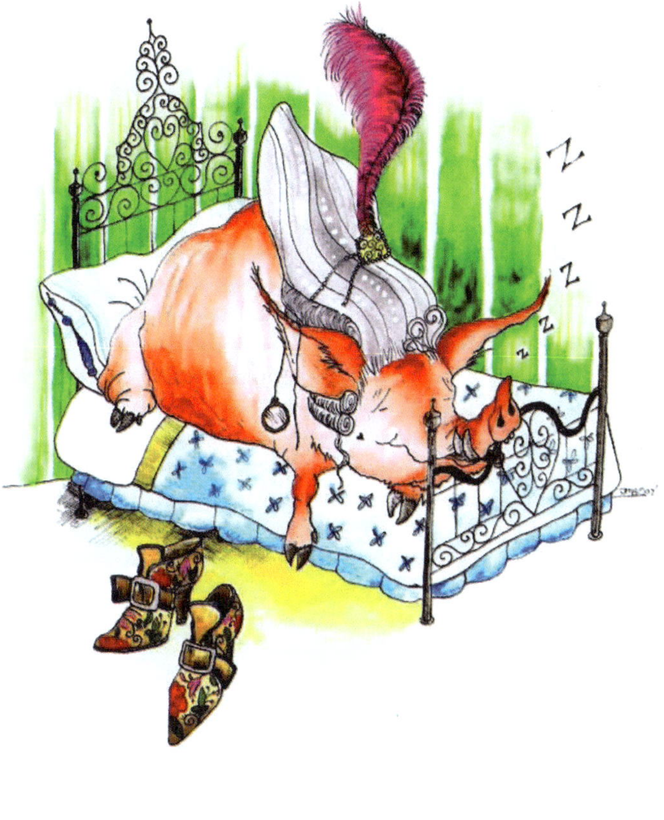

The pig in a wig
with the shoes
that are big
gets dressed for
the day in a
fine, natty rig.

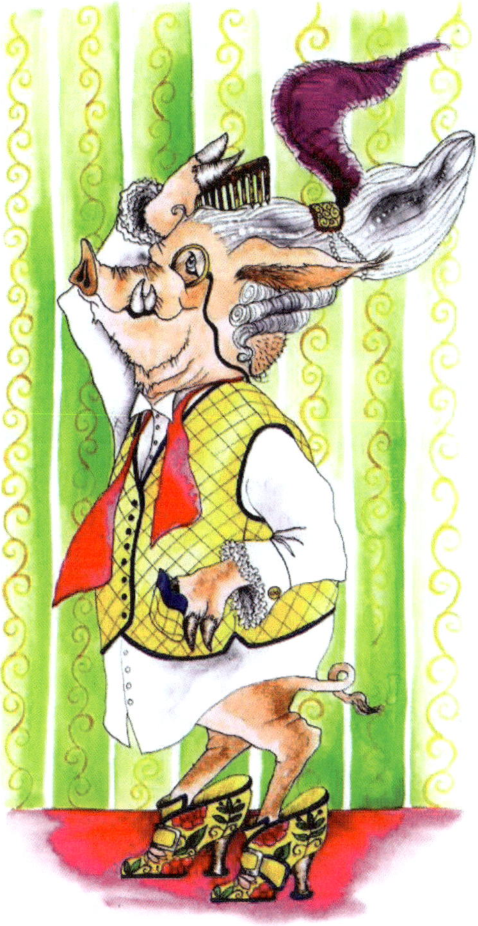

The pig with the
wig; the fine, natty
rig and the
shoes that are big,
takes a lively
spin in his
two-wheeled
gig.

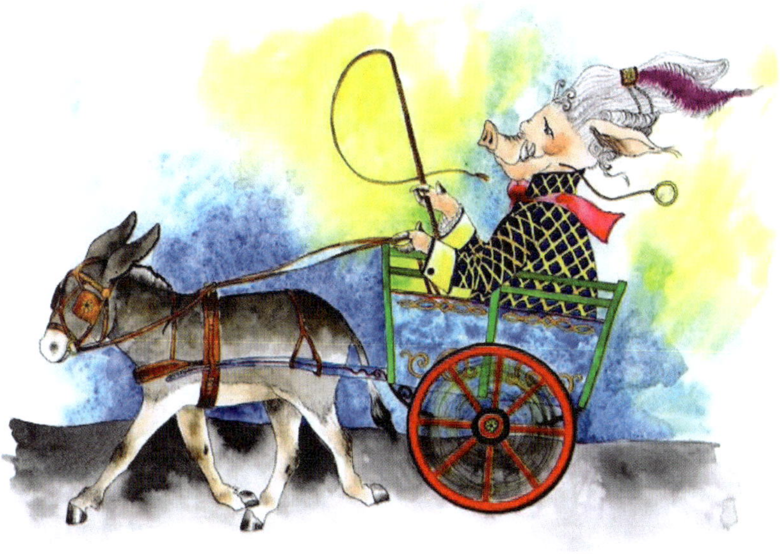

A gig for a pig with his rig and his wig — and his shoes that are big — drives back home; what a fine, handsome prig!

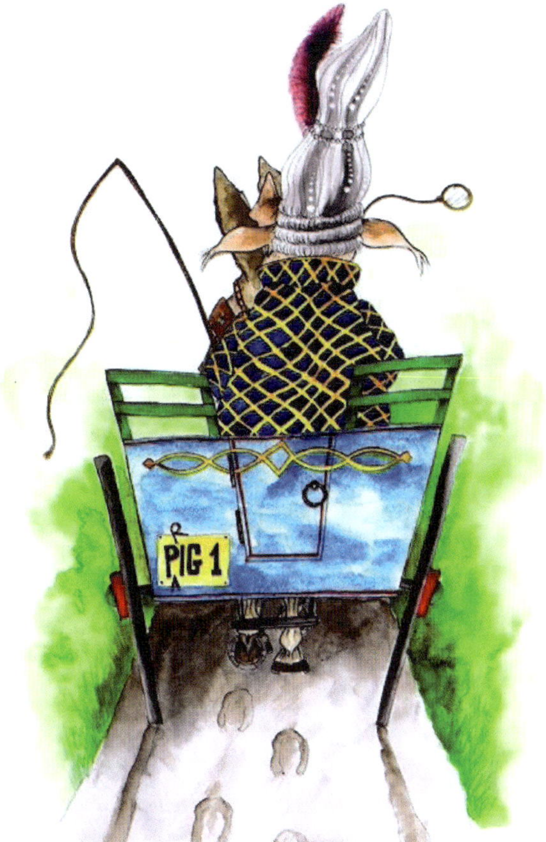
PIG 1

An afternoon passed clearing weed and twig; his asparagus patch needs a careful dig. The shoes that are big help the pig to dig,

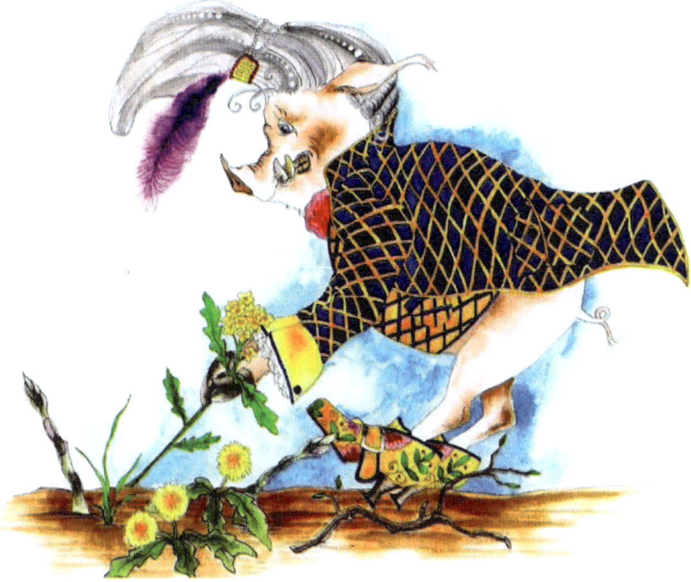

but he gets
quite warm in
that great fuzzy
wig.

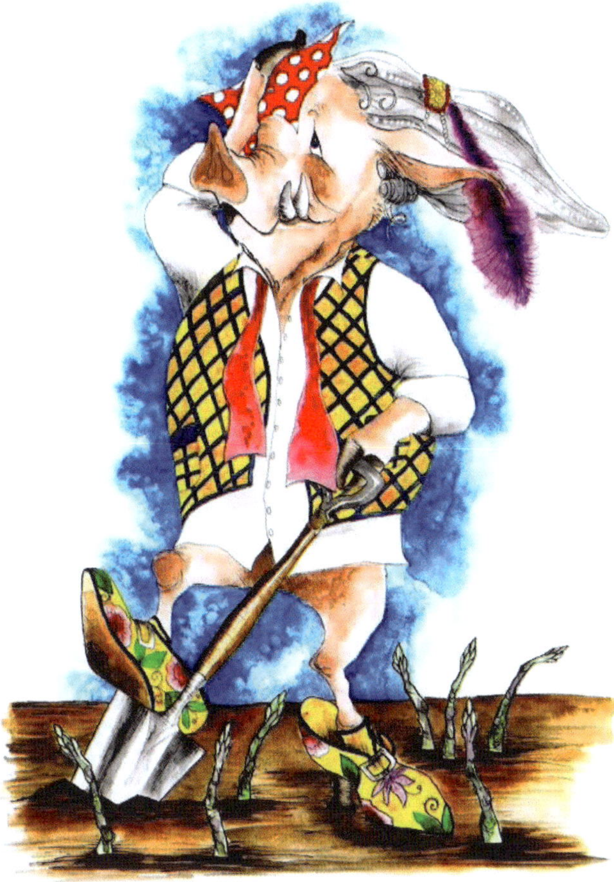

A bath before tea for a hot smelly pig! He takes off his wig and his fine, natty rig and enjoys a soak with his two-masted brig.

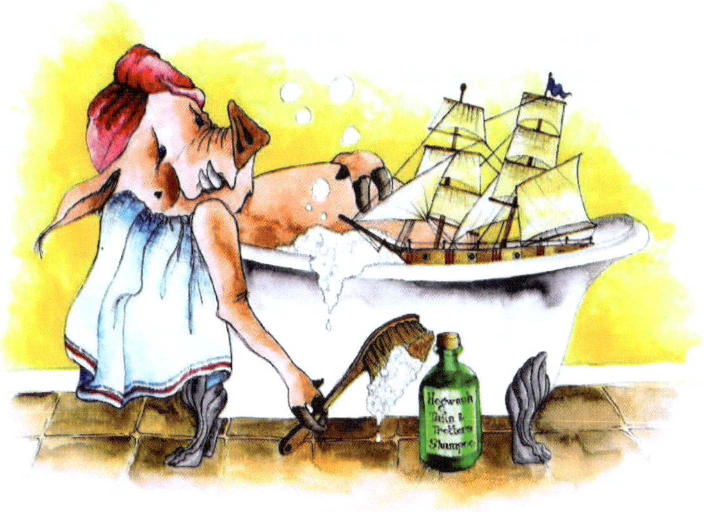
Hogwash

He dines alone on syrup and fig. Fig for a pig in his great fuzzy wig, then cordial downed with a delicate swig.

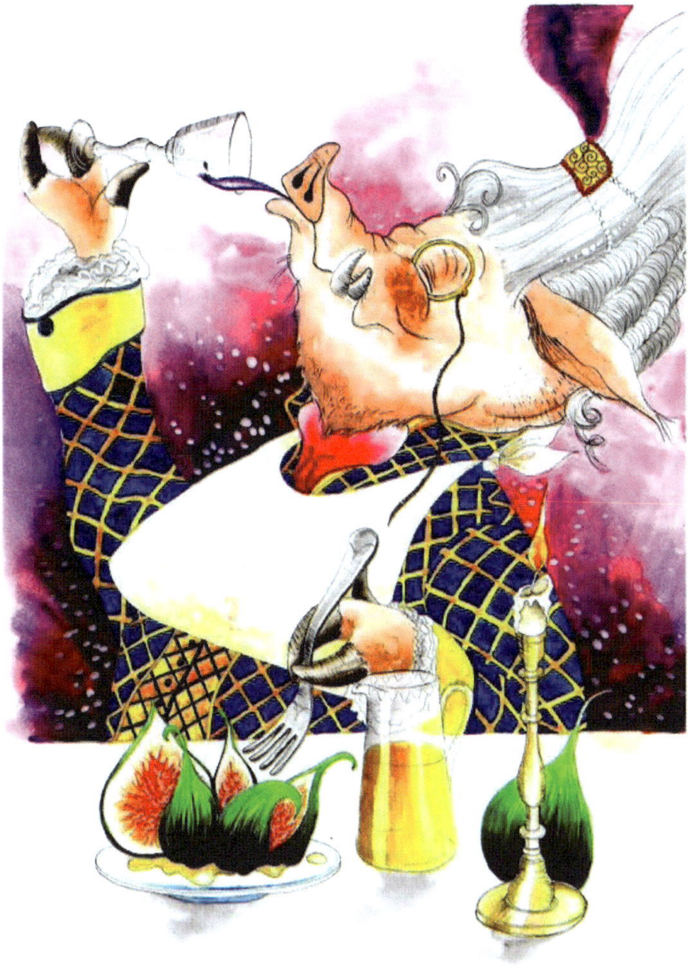

By the light of the moon, the satisfied pig taps his trotters inside the shoes that are big.

With a pluck on his fiddle and a primp of his wig, he feels happy enough to dance a light jig.

That handsome prig; that pig in a wig (full of cordial swig) dancing his jig all full up with fig!

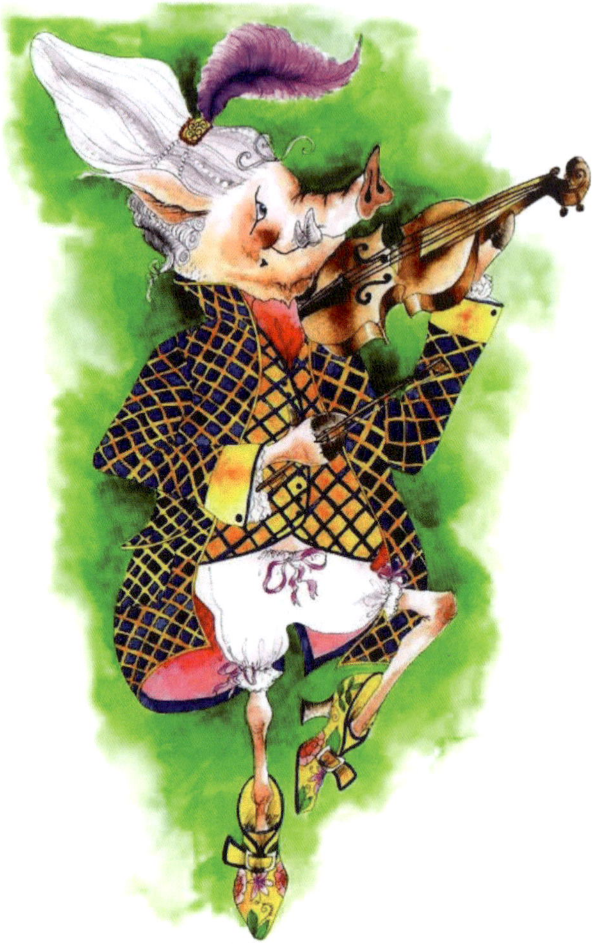

At midnight he takes off his fine, natty rig. In a bed that is small lies the fine, fat pig. He dreams of his trip in the two-wheeled gig — with the wind in his wig — and snores content on his syrup and fig.

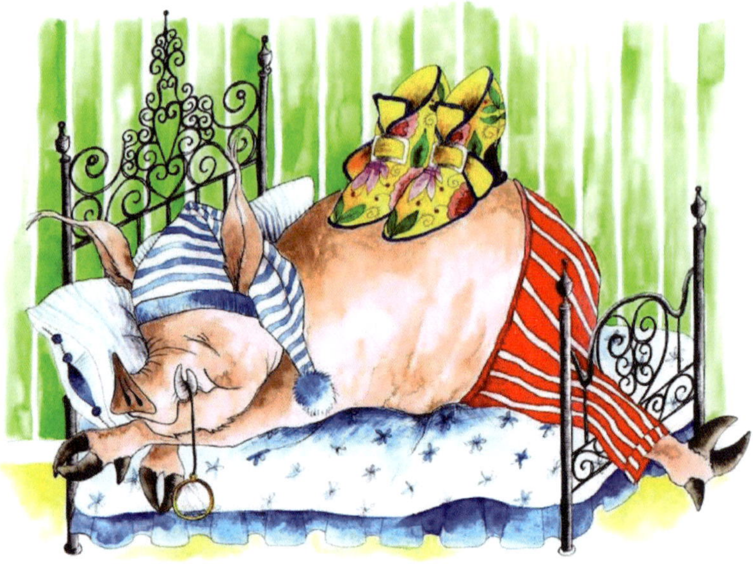

Placed side by side are the shoes (that are big), and still in the bath sails two-masted brig.

Printed in Great Britain
by Amazon